Pick a Plate

by Charis Mather

BEARPORT
PUBLISHING

Minneapolis, Minnesota

Credits

All images are courtesy of Shutterstock.com, unless otherwise specified. With thanks to Getty Images, Thinkstock Photo, and iStockphoto. Front Cover – Little Works, Poi NATTHAYA, Zvezdesign, Iconic Bestiary, Gaidamashchuk, Sudowoodo, ONYXprj, GoodStudio. Background – Little Works. 3 – Sudowoodo, Andrii Symonenko, ONYXprj. 6–9 – Designation, 21kompot, KutuzovaDesign, mayalis, Ramcreative, SeekandFind, Katy Flaty, Sudowoodo, Akane1988, Dernkadel, Designation, Dustick, GoodStudio, Pretty Vectors, SThom, Viktoria Sokolova. 10–13 – BeataGFX, kostolom3000, Montae, Mountain Brothers, Neliakott, stockakia. 14–17 – Jonasan Kesuken, lukpedclub, mything, Reinbow Cake. 18–21 – Ienjoyeverytime, Natalllenka.m, svtdesign, Neliakott, KutuzovaDesign. 22&23 – BeataGFX, kostolom3000, Montae, Mountain Brothers, Neliakott, stockakia, Jonasan Kesuken, lukpedclub, mything, Reinbow Cake, Natalllenka.m, KutuzovaDesign

Library of Congress Cataloging-in-Publication Data is available at www.loc.gov or upon request from the publisher.

ISBN: 979-8-88509-351-4 (hardcover)
ISBN: 979-8-88509-473-3 (paperback)
ISBN: 979-8-88509-588-4 (ebook)

For more information, write to Bearport Publishing, 5357 Penn Avenue South, Minneapolis, MN 55419.

CONTENTS

What Is in Your Lunch? 4

Food Groups: So Much to Choose! 6

Some of Everything 8

Hot Dog OR Soup and Salad? 10

Baked Potatoes OR Mac and Cheese? 14

Fish Stick Sandwich OR Tuna Wrap? 18

Food for Thought 22

Glossary 24

Index 24

WHAT IS IN YOUR LUNCH?

What do you want to eat for lunch? Do you like sandwiches, pasta, or pizza? Eating lunch is an important way for our bodies to get **energy** for the rest of the day.

Our lunches are made up of different kinds of food that help our bodies in different ways. Getting the right amounts of each kind of food keeps our bodies **healthy** and strong.

FOOD GROUPS
SO MUCH TO CHOOSE!

There are five main groups of food.

Fruits

Foods in this group can be fresh, frozen, or from a can. Eat fruits of many different colors.

Vegetables
These parts of plants help keep us healthy in many ways. It's good to have different kinds on your plate.

Grains

This group has rice, wheat, and other plant seeds. It also has all the foods made from grains, such as bread and pasta.

Protein

Fish, meat, chicken, eggs, peas, nuts, and beans all have protein.

MILK

Dairy

This group has milk, cheese, and yogurt. It also includes soy milk and soy yogurt.

SOME OF EVERYTHING

Every day, your body needs food from all five groups. This plate shows a **balanced** meal. It can help you have the right kinds of food in the right amounts. Aim to have this balance during your day.

It's okay to eat foods from different groups at different meals.

Fruits

Vegetables

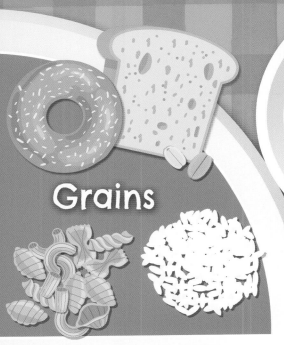

Grains

Dairy

MILK

Protein

We should eat veggies, fruits, and grains the most. Foods that have a lot of fat or added sugar can be bad for our bodies. Try to skip them.

Can you pick the plates that have a good balance of food groups?

HOT DOG

Hot dog meat has protein, which our bodies need to grow and stay strong. But this meat often has a lot of fat, too. Hot dog buns are made from grains, which give us energy.

Ketchup has lots of sugar. Eating too much sugar is not good for our bodies.

OR SOUP AND SALAD?

Soup and salad are both made with vegetables. Different veggies help our bodies in different ways. Some keep us from being tired and sick.

Which **plate** would **YOU** pick?

Which plate did you pick? Hot dogs have more fat than we need, and ketchup adds sugar. The soup and salad meal has healthy veggies. Still, we can make both better!

Try a kind of meat with less fat, such as a turkey hot dog.

Whole grain buns have more healthy **nutrients** than white buns.

Add some fresh veggies for taste and crunch.

For some protein, add meat or tofu to your soup and salad.

Salad dressings can have a lot of sugar and fat. You only need a little bit to add flavor.

Put many kinds of veggies in your salad.

BAKED POTATOES

Potatoes are veggies that have lots of **potassium** (puh-TA-see-um). This helps keep our hearts healthy. Sometimes, baked potatoes are topped with foods from other groups, such as meat or cheese.

OR MAC AND CHEESE?

This plate includes lots of milk and cheese, which are from the dairy food group. Dairy helps keep our bones strong.

Macaroni noodles are made from grains.

Which plate would YOU pick?

Which plate did you pick? The mac and cheese has more dairy than we need in one meal. A baked potato can be a good start to a balanced lunch. Let's make both plates better!

Eat fresh veggies with your baked potatoes.

Try adding less meat and cheese. We should eat more veggies than meat or dairy.

Add broccoli or other veggies to your mac and cheese.

Try using whole grain noodles.

Use less cheese in your macaroni meal to have less fat.

17

FISH STICK SANDWICH

Fish has healthy protein. But **fried** fish sticks are cooked in fatty oil. Fried foods often have more fat than we need.

Exercise can help our bodies use up extra fat.

OR TUNA WRAP?

This plate has a few food groups. The tuna fish has protein, and the tortilla it's wrapped in is made from grains. The wrap is full of yummy veggies, too!

Which **plate** would **you** pick?

Which plate did you pick? Both meals have protein and grains, but the tuna wrap also has vegetables. How can we make both plates better?

Add fresh veggies to your fish sandwich.

Baking fish sticks instead of frying them will take out some of the fat.

Use whole grain bread.

To add some dairy, have a glass of milk with your lunch.

Choose a whole wheat tortilla for your wrap.

21

FOOD FOR THOUGHT

Now, you know more about balanced meals. Can you choose your own healthy lunch? Remember to pick foods from different groups.

Be creative!
There are so many different foods to try.

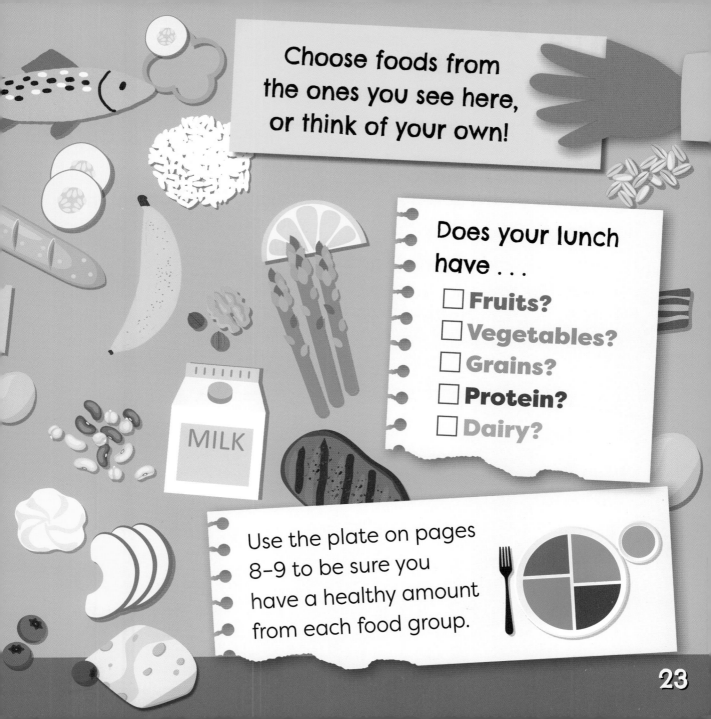

Choose foods from
the ones you see here,
or think of your own!

Does your lunch
have . . .

☐ **Fruits?**
☐ **Vegetables?**
☐ **Grains?**
☐ **Protein?**
☐ **Dairy?**

Use the plate on pages
8–9 to be sure you
have a healthy amount
from each food group.

MILK

GLOSSARY

balanced the right amount of things

energy the power to be able to do things

fried cooked in hot oil

healthy when the body is working well and is not sick

nutrients things in food that people need to grow and be healthy

potassium a nutrient that your body needs to stay healthy

INDEX

bread 7, 20

cheese 7, 14-17

dairy 7, 9, 15-16, 23

fat 9, 12-13, 18, 20

fried 18-19

meat 7, 10, 12-14, 16

nutrients 12

oil 18

protein 7, 9-10, 13, 18, 20, 23

vegetables 6, 8-9, 11-12, 14, 16-17, 19-20, 23